STUBBY

BRAVE SOLDIER DOG

By Richard and Sally Glendinning

Illustrated by Richard Amundsen

GARRARD PUBLISHING COMPANY
CHAMPAIGN, ILLINOIS

STUBBY
BRAVE SOLDIER DOG

The little brindle and white dog was tired and hungry. He had walked for a long time, and his paws were sore. It was a hot day in August 1917. The little dog was thirsty. He was panting, and his pink tongue hung outside his mouth. He was lost. It seemed to him that he had been lost for a long time.

Then his ears perked up. Ahead of him were long rows of tents. The little dog went closer. He saw hundreds of young men. The men were soldiers, and they were wearing the light brown uniform of the United States army. They were in the Yankee Division, training on the campus of Yale University in New Haven, Connecticut. The little dog liked the soldiers' faces. Maybe one of the soldiers would be his friend and give him a place to stay.

A soldier whistled to him. "Come on, doggie," the soldier called. The little dog went closer, and the soldier picked him up. The dog's short tail wagged, and he trembled with joy as the soldier patted his head.

4

The other soldiers smiled as they watched him. "He's not much more than a puppy," one of them said. "He looks like a little Boston terrier, but he's mostly mutt."

"What do you suppose his name is?" asked another.

"There's no way of telling," said the soldier who held the dog in his arms. "He has a little collar around his neck, but there's no name tag on it."

The dog wagged his short tail so hard it went thump, thump, thump against his new friend's chest. The soldier laughed. "With a tail as short as that, he ought to be called Stubby."

From that time on, the little dog was known as Stubby.

Stubby liked the soldiers and their camp. He tried to be very good so that the soldiers would let him stay. The camp soon became his home.

Stubby's special friend was the tall soldier who had whistled to him first. The soldier's name was J. Robert Conroy, and the other soldiers called him Bob. Stubby wanted to follow Bob everywhere. He would trot along, his tail wagging.

"No, no, Stubby," Bob would sometimes say. "You can't come with me now. Stay in the tent."

Then Stubby would curl up and take a nap on his little mat.

There was a rule against having pets in the camp, for they might get in the way of training drills. The soldiers were

7

training to fight a great war in Europe. But the officers were kind men, so they pretended not to see Stubby. Sometimes an officer would stop and pet him. He would talk to Stubby about his own dog back home.

As the days went by, Stubby became more and more used to army life. He awakened when the bugle blew each morning. He went outside to watch the soldiers raise the American flag to the top of the tall flagpole. He learned the meaning of all the bugle calls. The bugle call he liked best was the mess call, because that meant it was time to eat. Stubby had never eaten such good food. He grew bigger and stronger. Even his bark was louder.

Each day, Bob found time to brush Stubby's coat until it shone. Sometimes the soldiers put him in a washtub for a bath. Stubby didn't like that much, for the soapsuds got in his eyes.

The little dog worked hard to become a good soldier. He learned to stand at attention. He marched beside the band, almost in step with the music. He even learned to salute by sitting down and raising his right paw to his face. The soldiers called Stubby their mascot. The little dog had never been so happy. The camp had become his home, and he wanted to stay there forever.

One day Stubby found that a change had come over the camp. No one spoke to him or patted him. None of the soldiers smiled. Stubby did not know what was going on. He lay with his nose over his paws and watched the soldiers.

The hundreds of tents were taken down and folded. Then they were loaded

on trucks or horse-drawn wagons. The soldiers packed their belongings in duffle bags. Now Stubby knew that his friends were getting ready to go somewhere. He ran from one soldier to another and begged them to take him with them.

Bob and another soldier stopped their work when Stubby came to them. Bob put his hand on Stubby's head. "Sorry, little fellow," he said softly. "We're moving out."

"I think he already knows," the other soldier said.

Bob nodded his head. "We are going overseas, Stubby," he said. "You can't go there with us."

Stubby whimpered, and his short ears drooped.

"Say, I've got an idea!" Bob said. "First, we have to go on the troop train. The train will take us to the port where the ship is waiting to carry us overseas. Maybe Stubby can go along with us that far."

The two soldiers laughed aloud. "Sure he can!" they shouted. Stubby liked that good sound of laughter.

So Stubby was carried aboard the train crowded with soldiers that headed south toward Virginia. He trotted down the aisle to visit all his friends. The soldiers played little games with him. They hid bits of food for him to find or tossed a red ball for him to catch in his mouth. Time passed more quickly while they played with Stubby. And he liked playing games.

The troop train arrived the next day at the seaport of Newport News. The soldiers and their duffle bags were loaded on the big steamship that was to sail for France that night. The soldiers couldn't bear to leave Stubby behind. He was quickly smuggled up the gangplank and hidden in a coal bin.

"Don't make any noise, Stubby!" a soldier whispered. "Stay!"

Stubby obeyed his orders. The coal bin was dark, but Stubby wasn't afraid. He knew his friends would come for him when they could. Some of the coal dust got in his nose, and he wanted to sneeze. He rubbed his paw against his nose and kept quiet. He stayed in his hiding place until the ship was far out to sea. When Bob came to get him, Stubby barked with joy.

"You're safe now, Stubby," Bob said. "We are so far out on the water that there is no way you can be sent back."

Stubby had the run of the ship. He explored every nook and cranny. He made friends with the sailors in the U.S. navy who ran the ship, but he still liked the soldiers best.

The weather was stormy, and heavy rain fell on the ship's decks. The ocean was rough. Big waves slapped against the sides of the ship, which rocked to and fro. Many of the soldiers and even the sailors felt ill from the endless rocking of the great vessel, but Stubby was never seasick.

After a few days, the storm ended. The sun shone once more, and the deep blue water of the ocean was calmer. Stubby went on deck to frolic around his new friends.

One of the soldiers was working on a present for Stubby. The man cut two circles from thin metal. He put Stubby's name on one piece of metal. On the other piece, he put Stubby's serial number. The man made up the number, because the little dog didn't have a real serial number as every soldier did.

The soldier fastened the two metal discs to Stubby's little collar. As far as Stubby and the soldiers were concerned, Stubby was now a real soldier. All of the soldiers had to wear these tags, which they called "dog tags." It was a good name for Stubby's tags. He wore them proudly.

After many days, the steamship docked in France. Bob worried about how he

would get Stubby off the ship. Officers would be watching closely at the foot of the gangplank. They would surely say that Stubby must be sent back to the United States.

Bob rolled Stubby up inside of an army blanket. That didn't work, for Stubby's plump body made a large lump in the blanket.

"All right, Stubby," Bob said. "We'll try another way. I'll wrap my overcoat around you. You must stay very quiet. Don't even wiggle."

Bob walked down the long gangplank with his heavy coat over his shoulder. Stubby was hidden inside the coat. Bob held him very tight.

A French army officer looked at the

heavy coat slung over Bob's shoulder. He seemed about to speak. But there were so many soldiers coming down the gangplank after Bob that the officer waved his arm. Bob and Stubby passed safely through! The soldiers began to smile and nudge each other in the ribs. They knew that their little pal would march beside them!

Stubby's dog tags flashed in the sun as he strutted proudly with the troops to their first camp in France. They were still far from the battlefield. The young soldiers in the Yankee Division knew no more about war than Stubby did. They knew, though, that this was serious and dangerous business. Stubby seemed to know that, too. This was not the time to romp and play. His duty was to stay with his friends in the Yankee Division. His little legs hurried to keep in step with the marching soldiers.

When the soldiers were settled in camp, Stubby kept busy. He helped Bob stand guard duty. He visited all his friends to cheer them up when they seemed sad. Stubby got lost three times and spent those nights away from camp, but he always found his way back. The soldiers joked about those times and said Stubby was "absent without leave." The soldiers would have been punished for that. Not Stubby, though. By now, he had won the heart of the chief officer, the colonel, who loved Stubby as much as all the soldiers did.

"Stubby is the only soldier who can talk back to me and get away with it," the colonel said.

The colonel chose Bob to carry important messages from headquarters to other places. Bob rode a horse through the woods and over rolling fields. Stubby ran along beside the horse until he got tired. Then Bob would stop. He would lift Stubby up to sit in front on the saddle. Stubby loved these adventures with Bob.

It was not always work. Sometimes Bob would be given a few days off. Then Stubby and Bob visited many of the French villages. One time they went to the little town where Joan of Arc was born. Joan of Arc was a brave woman who had led French soldiers in

battle many years before. Kind village people gave Stubby his very first medal. He was the only American soldier-dog they had ever seen.

After many weeks of hard training, the Yankee Division was ordered to the front. Now the soldiers had a new worry. What would happen to Stubby? He was the only American dog known to be overseas with the army troops. Would he be allowed to go with them into battle?

The colonel took care of that. "Stubby is going with the men," he said. He wrote out a special order that made the dog an official mascot of the Yankee Division.

Stubby reached the front lines of battle on February 5, 1918. He went along as his friends climbed down into deep trenches in the earth. The trenches would shelter them from the enemy's gunfire. Stubby learned to huddle quietly at the bottom of the trench as the shells exploded in the air above his head. For more than a month, Stubby and his friends were under fire night and day. He had never heard anything as loud as the sounds made by the big guns and the bursting shells. There was also the deep boom of the American cannons when they fired back. Stubby's ears hurt from the noise, but he tried not to be afraid.

Stubby learned that the sound of horns was a warning that the enemy was attacking with gas. This was a poison gas.

It came across the field in a quiet cloud and settled to the ground. The men feared it more than anything else, for they knew they would get sick if they breathed the poison gas. When the horns went off, the soldiers put gas masks over their faces to protect themselves from the gas. A soldier made a gas mask for Stubby, too, but it didn't fit very well. It was hard to fit the mask tightly over Stubby's face. In one attack, he got a whiff of the gas. It made him quite sick. This was the first time Stubby had been hurt in battle.

Soon Stubby was well again. He knew his soldier buddies needed him to cheer them up. He darted up and down the trenches with his little tail wagging just as if they were safe at home again. He stopped along the way, and the little dog brought smiles to the soldiers' faces.

Stubby was good at finding wounded soldiers. Even with bullets whizzing over his head, Stubby would dart out of the

trench and race about on the search.
When he found a hurt soldier on the
field, he would run back to get help.
Often he stayed with the wounded man
until the soldier was moved back to a
field hospital.

Stubby had never seen enemy soldiers until some of them were taken prisoner. Somehow he knew the difference between the enemy soldiers and the men on his own side. He growled deep in his throat when he saw them.

Very soon after that, Stubby was out in "no-man's-land." This was the wide stretch of ground that lay between the enemy's trenches and his own. He was looking for any of his buddies who might have been wounded in the fighting. He heard a strange sound in some nearby bushes and went to look. There, trying to hide, was an enemy soldier! The soldier did not see him.

Stubby crept toward the man. He tried to move quietly, but he could not keep back an angry growl. The man jerked his head around and saw Stubby coming at him. The man threw up his hands and said something Stubby could not understand. Then the man pretended he was a friend. Stubby knew better. Growling louder, he charged at full speed.

The man tried to run away toward his own trenches. Stubby raced after him and nipped at his heels. The man stumbled. In a flash, Stubby jumped up and grabbed him by the seat of the pants. The man tried to shake him loose, but Stubby had a bulldog's strong jaws. He dragged the man to a stop.

By now the enemy soldier was howling loudly. His yells brought several of Stubby's friends on the run.

"Look at that!" one of them shouted. "Stubby's caught himself a prisoner!"

"By the seat of the pants," another said. "All right, Stubby, you can let go now."

Stubby turned his prisoner over to his buddies. They hurried the man back to their side. With his head held high, Stubby trotted proudly behind.

Like all the other soldiers, Stubby was very tired. There was little time to rest, though. It seemed the fighting would never end. One day as he prowled into no-man's-land, he felt so tired he didn't think he could move another step. Suddenly a shell exploded near him. It was followed by a smell his keen nose quickly picked up. He knew what it was.

It was the smell of the gas that had made him so sick before.

Forgetting all about his weariness, Stubby raced like the wind for a friendly trench. He leaped down and saw one of his buddies lying in a deep sleep. The soldier was not wearing a gas mask. Stubby barked at him, but he couldn't awaken the man. Stubby grabbed the soldier's coat sleeve and shook it hard. Finally, the soldier opened his eyes.

"Gas!" the soldier cried. He quickly put on his gas mask and found Stubby's mask for him. The warning horns began to hoot. When the gas faded away, the soldier hugged Stubby. "Thanks, good buddy," he said. "You saved my life. I was too tired to wake up."

At last the day arrived when Stubby and his friends were replaced by fresh troops. The Yankee Division was moved a safe distance behind the front lines to get the rest it so badly needed. The men slept as much as they could. They also got a chance to take hot showers to wash off the mud of the trenches. Stubby was given a good scrubbing in a washtub. This time he didn't care if the soapsuds got in his eyes. It felt so good to have all the caked mud washed from his coat and paws.

There was a piano at the rest center. The men often gathered around it to sing songs that reminded them of home. Stubby joined in with them, with his head thrown back to howl at the ceiling.

Women of the American Red Cross also reminded the soldiers of home. The women mended torn uniforms and darned socks. They were ready to talk to a homesick young soldier or to help him write a letter to his family. They always had a good supply of hot coffee and doughnuts, and Stubby got more than his share of the doughnuts.

The rest period ended all too soon. The Yankee Division was ordered back to the front, although not to the same place where the earlier fighting had been. Now it rained most of the time. But the Yankee Division slowly began to push back the enemy.

After one battle, Stubby thought the enemy soldiers had gone. He crawled out of the trench to take a look around. He didn't know that a few of the enemy soldiers were still nearby. One of them threw a hand grenade. It exploded very close to Stubby. A piece of metal hit Stubby in the chest near his left foreleg. He let out a yelp of pain. Howling, he tried to drag himself back to the trench. He couldn't make it.

Bob raced to help his little friend. He gently cradled Stubby in his arms and carried the little dog back to a first-aid station. The doctor examined Stubby, and then shook his head.

"He's badly hurt," the doctor said. "He needs more than just some tape and a bandage."

Bob saw to it that Stubby was made

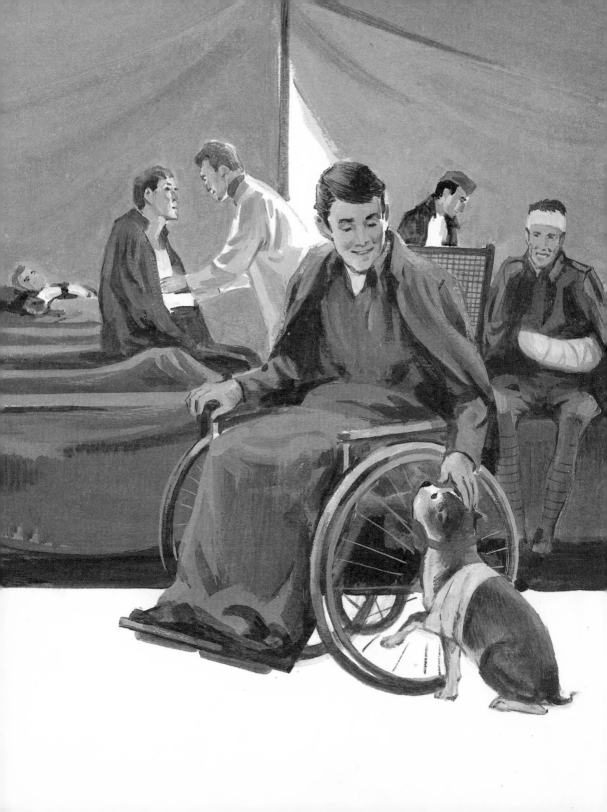

comfortable in an ambulance. Then Bob had to return to his headquarters while Stubby rode to the field hospital. There he was given the same good care that any wounded soldier would have had.

His strength came back very slowly. As soon as he was able, Stubby began to roam the halls and wards with a slight limp. His friendly manner won the hearts of everyone.

As far as the doctors and nurses were concerned, Stubby was welcome to stay forever. They could see how much good he was doing by cheering up their soldier patients. Stubby was glad to make new friends, but he missed his buddies at the front lines.

One day he heard a familiar voice in

the hall. It was Bob! Stubby raced to his friend. Bob had gotten special permission from the colonel to come to the hospital and get Stubby.

The great war ended on November 11, 1918. The enemy surrendered. When the

news reached the soldiers, they shouted
and danced with joy. Stubby danced
among them, his little tail wagging.
Never had he seen such excitement, and
he was a part of the victory. He had
served bravely in seventeen battles.

"It's all over, Stubby!" Bob cried. "The war is over!"

Stubby's tail wagged harder than ever. (Woodrow Wilson, the president of the United States, had come to Europe to help to work out the peace terms.) He decided to review the American troops. President Wilson was on the reviewing stand with the French leaders. The stand was bright with red, white, and blue bunting. American and French flags fluttered in the crisp breeze. Everyone was in a happy mood. The marching music of the military band set toes to tapping.

When the Yankee Division swung past the president, Stubby led the way. He was wearing a blanket of chamois—a fine, soft leather—that kind French

women had made for him. It was trimmed with the flags of the Allies. It gave Stubby's name and the name of his unit. Medals he had won were pinned on it. A gold stripe showed that he had been wounded in battle. Three other stripes told how long he had served. Stubby was proud to have his very own uniform. He passed the reviewing stand with his head held high. Everyone said he was a hero.

Many people smiled broadly as they watched Stubby in the parade. President Wilson was one of them. He wanted to meet this unusual, four-footed soldier. When Stubby was brought to him later, Stubby saluted and held out his paw to be shaken.

In April of 1919, Stubby returned with Bob to the United States. He had served overseas for nineteen months. This time he was not smuggled off the ship. He walked down the gangplank with his head held high. Everyone knew about him. He was guest of honor everywhere he went.

Bob entered him in a big dog show in Boston. The crowd was the largest the show had ever had. Many of the people came only to see Stubby. The owners of the show dogs did not want Stubby to be shown. Their dogs were purebreds. Stubby was only a mutt.

"He may be a mutt," said the judges, "but he's done more than all of your dogs put together. Stubby stays."

Not only did he stay, he won a gold medal for being a "Hero Dog."

The medal was pinned to his decorated blanket. Later, General John J. Pershing, the head of all the American armies, gave Stubby another gold medal from the Humane Education Society. This, too, was fastened to the blanket. Stubby was getting so many new medals and badges there seemed hardly room to put them all on the blanket.

Other honors came to him in the years after the war. He became a member of the American Legion and was a special guest at their conventions and banquets. He marched with them in their parades. He visited the White House and met President and Mrs.

Warren Harding. He also met President Calvin Coolidge. He became an honorary member of the American Red Cross. He was made a lifetime member in the Y.M.C.A. His membership card said that it was good for three bones a day and a place to sleep.

On March 16, 1926, Stubby found his final resting place. After a happy life, he died quietly in the arms of his loving master, Bob Conroy.

FOR MARJORIE COTTON

A HOLT REINFORCED EDITION
ISBN: 0-03-088370-9
Library of Congress Catalog Card Number: 79-155869
Printed in the United States of America / First American Edition,
March, 1972; Second Printing, November, 1973

WALTZING MATILDA

Poem by

A. B. Paterson

Illustrations by

Desmond Digby

Holt, Rinehart and Winston, Inc.

New York, Chicago, San Francisco

Oh! There once was a swagman camped in a Billabong,

Under the shade of a Coolabah tree;

And he sang as he looked at his old billy boiling,

"Who'll come a-waltzing Matilda with me?"

Who'll come a-waltzing Matilda, my darling,
Who'll come a-waltzing Matilda with me?
Waltzing Matilda and leading a water-bag—
Who'll come a-waltzing Matilda with me?

Down came a jumbuck to drink at the water-hole,

Up jumped the swagman and grabbed him in glee;

And he sang as he stowed him away in his tucker-bag,
"You'll come a-waltzing Matilda with me!"

Who'll come a-waltzing Matilda, *my darling*,

Who'll come a-waltzing Matilda with me?

Waltzing Matilda and leading a water-bag—

Who'll come a-waltzing Matilda with me?

Down came the Squatter a-riding his thoroughbred;

Down came Policemen—one,

two

and three.

"Whose is the jumbuck you've got in your tucker-bag?

You'll come a-waltzing Matilda with me."

Who'll come a-waltzing Matilda, my darling,
Who'll come a-waltzing Matilda with me?
Waltzing Matilda and leading a water-bag—
Who'll come a-waltzing Matilda with me?

But the swagman, he up and he jumped in the water-hole,

Drowning himself by the Coolabah tree;

And his ghost may be heard as it sings in the billabong,

"Who'll come a-waltzing Matilda with me?"

GLOSSARY

BILLABONG: A backwater from an inland river, sometimes returning to it and sometimes ending in sand. Except in floodtimes it is usually a dried-up channel containing a series of pools or waterholes.

BILLY: A cylindrical tin pot with a lid and a wire handle used as a bushman's kettle.

COOLABAH TREE: A species of *Eucalyptus*, *E. microtheca*, common in the Australian inland where it grows along watercourses.

JUMBUCK: A sheep. From an aboriginal word, the original meaning of which is obscure.

SQUATTER: Originally applied to a person who placed himself on public land without a license, it was extended to describe one who rented large tracts of Crown (state-owned) land for grazing and later to one who owned his sheep run.

SWAGMAN: A man who, carrying his personal possessions in a bundle or SWAG, travels on foot in the country in search of casual or seasonal employment. A tramp.

TUCKER-BAG: A bag used to carry food, especially by people traveling in the bush.

WALTZING MATILDA: Carrying a swag; possibly a corruption of "walking Matilda." "Matilda" was a type of swag where the clothes and personal belongings were wrapped in a blanket roll and tied toward each end like a party cracker. The roll was carried around the neck with the loose ends falling down each side in front, one end clasped by the arm.

ABOUT THE AUTHOR

A. B. PATERSON was born at Narrambla, New South Wales, Australia, in 1864. He became a lawyer and was still practicing when he began to write ballads that were published in the Sydney *Bulletin*. He wrote "Waltzing Matilda," which was to become practically an Australian national anthem, to the tune of an old English marching song. Paterson later became a journalist and also wrote two novels and a book of verse for children. Several collections of his verse were successfully published in Australia. He died in Sydney in 1941.

ABOUT THE ARTIST

DESMOND DIGBY is a satirical painter and theatrical designer under contract to the Australian Opera Company. Of his illustrations for children's books he says, "I think of each page as a little set. I like miniatures, probably because of my theatrical work where I do strips and strips of sketches and choose the ones to be blown up later. I did some drawings for *Waltzing Matilda* and I didn't like them, so I tore them up. I work like that all the time —it has to be right for me, I'm afraid."

Waltzing Matilda is the second book which Mr. Digby has illustrated for children. He makes his home in Sydney.